G000161014

FLIRTING WITH TIGERS

First published in 2023 by
The Dedalus Press
13 Moyclare Road
Baldoyle
Dublin D13 K1C2
Ireland

www.dedaluspress.com

Copyright © Amy Abdullah Barry, 2023

ISBN 978-1-915629-09-8 (paperback)
ISBN 978-1-915629-08-1 (hardback)

All rights reserved.
No part of this publication may be reproduced in any form
or by any means without the prior permission
of the publisher.

The moral rights of the author have been asserted.

Dedalus Press titles are available in Ireland
from Argosy Books (www.argosybooks.ie) and in the UK
from Inpress Books (www.inpressbooks.co.uk)

Cover image artwork by Gaetano Tranchino,
by kind permission.
www.gaetanotranchino.com

Printed in Dublin by Print Dynamics.

The Dedalus Press receives financial assistance from
The Arts Council / An Chomhairle Ealaíon.

FLIRTING WITH TIGERS

AMY ABDULLAH BARRY

DEDALUS PRESS

ACKNOWLEDGEMENTS

The author wishes to thank the publishers and editors of the following magazines, journals and websites where a number of these poems, or earlier versions of them, originally appeared: *Cyphers, The Sunday Tribune, The Blue Nib, Sparks of the Everyday: Poetry Ireland Introductions 2022, Paris Lit Up, Sungurlu Newspaper Culture, Turkem Dergisi* (Kosovo), *Autumn Leaves, Roscommon Herald, Westmeath Independent, Atunis Journal* (Belgium), *The Poets' Republic, Where are you from* (New York), *Mary Evans Picture Library, Maryevan Poetry Blog, Live Encounters, Misty Mountain, Beneath Western Skies, The Galway Review, A New Ulster* and *The Storms*.

I wish to extend my deepest appreciation and special thanks to Thomas McCarthy who offered mentorship along the way. For words of encouragement, I am indebted to Jean O'Brien, Annemarie Ní Churreáin, Jessica Traynor, Anthony Anaxagorou and Jane Clarke.

Special thanks as well to Michael Barry, Yasmine Barry, Natasya Barry and Pablo.

Thank you to Pat Boran, Dedalus Press, and to artist Gaetano Tranchino for the cover artwork.

Contents

~

5

to Papa

The Breath of the Rainforest

We've set up the tent,
pale yellow powdered sulphur round its perimeter
to halt the slithering of snakes.

The ash-glow of the sky,
the wind howling into night,
are all in my mind.
I lie, open-eyed on a sleeping mat,

printing images in my head,
collecting the echoes of jungle creatures –
tarsiers, toucans, tigers,
wild elephants trumpeting troubles
from miles across the forest floor.

In the morning
the cinnamon air draws me out.
Sunlight hammers jagged patterns
through layers of Meranti leaves.

Everyone dives into the river,
its sepia water like the Teh tarik in my cup.
I head to the fern bushes
to find the blooming Rafflesia.

A growl from the woody beams of bamboo,
and I am squatting eye to eye with a boar.
Its skin is shiny-black, rough and thick,
designed for fighting.

And I am ready. My own skin
thickens in a breathless second.
Startled, the animal vanishes. I pin
the breath of the rainforest on my skin.

I Unfold My Own Myth

1945, the Malaysian jungle,
one sweltering afternoon, my uncle,
a twenty-year-old soldier, surrounded
by three Japanese from the Imperial Army,
their machine guns pointing directly at him.
Through his tears, two huge tigers appear,
to send them running for cover.
Then they are gone in seconds.
He, unharmed and assured.

My eldest sister, alone at home one evening.
A bang from downstairs,
heavily pregnant, she rises slowly from the bed,
whispers in the darkness: 'Please God, I beg your protection.'
Two tigers with lustrous fur appear like long-tooth angels,
guard either side of the door.
She doubles back.
She stands frozen. Baffled.
Later the tigers vanish completely.

Three decades after Grandpa died,
Papa told me he had a special gift:
Protector of his descendants in moments of distress.
When I was three, two tigers emerged
on Grandpa's headstone,
just sitting there as if it was natural,
like rocks by the side of a stream.

And yet, last December,
no tigers appeared when my brother was assaulted
by men who worship violence.
So how does this work?
Maybe they're still travelling thousands of miles
across lakes, hills, oceans, snow and bog –
just to get to me.

The Mango Tree

Today I picked mangoes
from a shelf in Tesco.
I used to gather them, yellowish-red,
from the ground
below drooping branches.

Above me, my brother, Jojo, climbed,
provoked to a manic dance
by red ants biting his feet.
He'd shake the mangoes off the tree,
and when he came down,
we'd carry them in a bamboo basket,
twenty steps to the front door.

Under the pergola,
I'd take one,
slice lengthwise
and crosswise,
invert each half.
The flesh stuck out
like the quills of a hedgehog.
We'd scoop it up,
to prepare cold smoothies, tangy and sweet,
relief from the heat for a day or two.

Jojo doesn't climb anymore,
but still, he talks of those ants.

All I have is an apple tree now,
whose fruits are so sour
I must smother them in sugar
to taste.

Taste of Penang

Two large mesh covers,
weighed down with glass beads
to guard the spread of food
from spiralling flies.

Mama looks to my sisters and me:
'Wash your hands before eating,
and remember to use the right,
to bring food to your mouth.
the left, for unsavoury tasks,
use only for the bathroom.'

After the evening azan prayer, I watch her
chopping, squeezing, mulching, pounding;
turmeric, galangal and dried chilies,
paring the skin of crab and cuttlefish,
as she sways about her space in the kitchen,
gold bangles clanging at her wrist.

She cooks by estimation,
not measurement,
feeling her way through a recipe,
cumin, coriander and cardamom
simmering in the wok,
Asian spices drift in the air.

'Remember...Cook for love,' she says,
'or there will be no flavour at all.'
After the tableware is settled,

we lift the corners of the net,
its beads shivering
like a distant prayer.

Off-roading in the Malaysian Jungle

A Jeep bumping through the wet jungle,
luggage bound tight to the roof.
Omar smiles behind the wheel.
Days of adventure ahead.

Brake. Engine. Silence.

He touches a tiny leech on his cheek,
green-red, like earth and blood together.
Into his vast skin, it disappears.
Blood oozes in its wake.

I have read of such blood hunters,
their dark meandering into the chambers of human flesh
churning up fevers, vomiting, pain.
Although I fear for Omar,
I am grateful he has been chosen and not me.

Ruby, a chain-smoking doctor
who grins more than she speaks,
draws on her cigarette,
as it burns lazy orange in her left hand,
holds Omar's face firm with the right.
She proceeds to cut his face with exquisite care.

More blood.
A silence,
except for the grunting monkeys.
She removes the wriggling leech on the blade,

carefully flings it to the ground;
Quickly, skilfully, she stitches the wound.
We breathe deeper
on the woody cinnamon of air –

Watch the bloody little creature
quiver on the brown mud below,
almost grinning, showing its teeth.

At Grandma's

On stilts, a house above the sea.

Shoeless, I enter,
with betel kisses on both cheeks,
constant sounds of cooking from her kitchen.

We gaze out to the horizon,
slapped by the low tide's stench,
and the pungent scent of tobacco.
'Soon we have to move to the land.
The government wants to develop this place.'
She spits hard on the wood
of the jetty below her.

A skinny tomboy,
together with my cousins,
I plunge into jade waters,
poach cockles from the fishermen's cages,
ignoring grandma's screams up above.

On the creaking veranda,
we grill our catch
dipping them in peanut sauce,
sea breeze drying our hair.

Next day, time to leave.
After a flurry of kisses,
she stands framed in the open door,
tiny in her floral Nyonya blouse.
Her hair is sun-baked sand,
her curls white-tipped waves.

She blows cheroot smoke
with a regal air,
that follows us
back to dry land.

Champaca

Mama used to sit on a low stool,
stoking charcoal after morning prayer,
baking moist sweetened bread for breakfast.
The raisins inside it spiralled
like swirling patterns on a tree bark,
her oven a hefty aluminium pot,
four times bigger than a cake pan
filled with sand to balance the heat.

One morning, when I came to help,
her sarong was soaked,
red from the waist,
twisted like a wilting hibiscus.

The hospital doors opened with a gust of antiseptic.
My brother and I peeped into ICU.
'Come in…' mama waved,
hurried in her speech.
We dashed to her side,
but a nurse took us from her,
we sat in silence and prayed.
'Please God, make mama's pain go away.'

Most evenings now, papa walks in the garden
alone. Where the oven used to stand
the air is filled with sweet champaca,
the scent mama used to wear on her hair.

*Champaca is a Malay name for Magnolia.

Rain

'Rain brings good luck,' Papa would say.
 I need it now,
 through the blur of half-remembered prayers.

Spider legs of rain
crawling across
the hospital window.

My name being called.

Again   and

Again.

My mind is numb, displaced.
My body, swaddled
with a deathly ache.

A tanned Italian in a white coat,
holds a folder bearing my name
reassures me with a single word: 'Bene!'

Out on the street,
a busker strains his rocker's throat,
singing 'I don't wanna die.'

I stand at a distance
and sing with his song.
His hair like tar in the pulsing rain.

I breathe again.
I feel papa's presence
in a fresh, earthy air.

Ripe

From miles away I smell them,
sharp and bittersweet, hanging from branches,
unhatched in thorny shells.

In a Malay ritual, for forty-four days after giving birth,
I'm confined, cared for by my sister.
I bathe in lemongrass and pandan water.

She prepares medicinal plants,
ginger, turmeric and other spices,
the sweet fat of durian forbidden.

That was another world.
Now I'm craving it again,
thousands of miles from home.

My daughter buys frozen durians
from the Asian shop. She, too, has ripened,
is firm as the fruit we share.

Someday I'll tell her the Malay saying,
'When the durians come down, the sarongs
will soon come off.' Until then
I imagine the silky custard taste of the fruit
even in my sleep.

*Durian is regarded the King of fruits in Asia.

Farewell Mama

The constant pounding
of chillies, lemongrass and shallots,
where Mama assembles ingredients
in the kitchen, making
the kind of magic
I read in books of fairy tales.

Eagerly I look on –
bubbling pots of spicy beef curry,
an oven pregnant with crisp chicken,
fluffy rice white as a bride's dress,
pretty in patterned bowls.

Mama, a traditionalist, reminds me,
'Take these recipes with you,
and share them with others –
you are writing
a piece of our history, you know.'

In hellish heat and mumbled prayers,
I stare at the freshly turned earth,
heavy with the scent of white plumeria.

Lucky, the stray dog, mama used to feed,
somehow made it here
across miles of road to a cemetery,
to bark his whimpering farewell.

Tsunami

I journeyed in the dark,
wet cold air roped my body.
My ears burned.
My blood rushed

to the anguished cries
of slow death.
I felt trapped
and almost dead myself.

All around me, faces
wore garish masks,
like characters in a tragic opera,
desperate to rekindle hope.

Delhi

I've missed the train to Delhi.

In a wintry hostel room piled
with Lonely Planets, backpackers
unfolding maps as they shiver and smoke,
I choke on sour air, fleas fastened to my flesh
till it sprouts shiny colonies of blood.

Sunrise: the train arrives.

The stationmaster parades two teeth
to the east and west of his gum.
The crowd surges forward.
I wonder how trains take all our weight,
if someone will fall to the tracks.

Onward: in cabins.

People are sleeping,
their mouths open, swallowing shadows.
My neck bends, offering my head
and all its affairs
to the soft plain of my palm.

The train snubs nameless stations.

I reach into my rucksack,
wrapped in words.
It is Delhi comes over the horizon
to unwrap me.

Chang Cheng

a tribute to the Great Wall

Every stone is a story.

Leaning over the railing,
I'm clothed to the waist in bricks.
The trail meanders over hills,
twists down into darker forms.

Bodies straining,
hands and backs,
muscles rippling in the sunlight,
absorbing the bluster of a storm.

'Chang Cheng', they called it,
the long wall,
or 'The Long Graveyard,'
for the millions who perished
building it, their stories
as quiet, as undeniable as stone.

Izmir, An Eastern Gem

In Kordon pavement café,
Turkish coffee murmurs
on a hot bed of sand,
we savour in tiny fincan cups.

The scent of Izmir roams like a cat.

A Hundred Times

From the hurried morning
of my death, between
the sky and the horizon,
I saw my bed still unmade.

Distracted by the wonders
of sheep's bit, lamb's ear, sneeze weeds.
Bird song, to my ears,
was like a taunt.

Pinned to the ground,
my heart pushed against my ribs.
A man's fingers digging into me,
day dark with his eclipse.

The sound of my own voice
a hundred times around me,
and, on a beach, I lay
on sand scorched black.

Layers of crushed shells,
underneath my skin,
I left my twelve-year-old body,
calm as a robin singing in a field.

Madam Cartomancer

for Tita

Her hand spreading her silk scarf,
its pattern cracked like canai bread,
flat upon the table.
Our dining room,
her place of business.

One afternoon,
we sat on the other side of her scarf,
drew cards with cryptic images.
Tita's card was the Knight of Cups
a shining armour on a white charger.
Mine had the image of a boat.

'You're heading towards a future
in another country,' she told me,
'and you'll go into business soon.'

Tita's eyebrows spoke
a kind of shorthand.
In them, I read her thoughts: 'nonsense'.
But she became the sister-in-law of a king,
while I forged a living in oil and gas.

Here, in the Irish countryside –
stacked stones walls,
hawthorn hedges,
baling hay,

hay-bale jumping,
turf cutting,
gorse,
nettles,
coltsfoot,
rabbits, deer, cows, sheep
and slurry!

I find my nonsense in this country living.

A New Woman

The unruliness of my father's world –
women, monies, psychedelics –
colliding with hers, a captive
in a stone mansion,
haunted by his lustful pursuits.

He breaks her,
then he breaks me too.

Today
I stand over my father,
encased in pine.
How strange to see him
coffined and hideous,
ready to join
the mere chain of bones.

With dark hair swept
into the perfect bun
under a hat,
Mother in black,
looks years younger.

The sweet, freshly turned earth
smells like a beginning.

A Himalayan Bus Ride

The bus piles on ever more people.
Bodies thrust from all sides,
someone's bum against mine,
mingled limbs, merging clothes,
breath and body odour.

Some sit on top, like how mum
used to stuff our clothes into a suitcase
while I sat on it, squeezing
the latches closed.

Now the bus restarts, jerks,
struggles with its load, my face
lodged under the armpit of a tall,
bearded man. I pull in
my stomach and hold my breath.

Outside – I bend to squint –
terraced farms on the sloping hills,
my eyes lift to embrace
the snow-robed Himalayas.

At Ferringhi Beach, Penang

In the sweating air,
racing rainbow kites
colour the sky
like rainforest birds.

A ruby hibiscus behind my ear,
a batik flowing,
soft blown palms swaying,
ancient beach oaks swirling.

Naked on a bamboo mat,
deft hands work nutmeg oil
into tired nerves;
above me, a zebra dove singing.

Between Captivity and Villa Maria

The cracked olive on ancient farmlands,
Pink cactus blossoms,
Exhibit their soft wares.
Masserie are hot beds –
And we are expected to play.

Bathed in sweat,
We dance, swayed
By *la terra magica;*
We've tasted wine and cheese,
Tapas like pleasure girls.

We prowl the Mediterranean shore,
Wild and awake –
Strangers, almost lovers
on neutral ground.

Lovesick
And never free,
Sometimes
We forget all vows.

Betrayal in Rome

I want to experience places and people long gone,
to be so close to the past
that it could draw my blood.

And so I am here,
where gladiators, slaves and convicts
perished for the pleasure of the crowd.

This city breathes in dried dust under the midday sun,
cobbled streets twisted through its heart,
ivy scabbed on its buildings.

But I am in love
with traces of things that were here before us,
so I shun the Trevi fountain and all its shiny coins.

Maybe it's the heat,
but my thoughts grow heavier,
and every tourist in summer clothes is an imposter.

Tourism seems a betrayal of the past,
and, facing the Forum one evening, I'm sure I hear
Caesar whisper, 'Et tu, Brute?'

Rain on the River Suck

For once, I don't have
to look at my watch. You talk,
relive memories of the river.

The dark water sparkles
in the moonlight, reeds sway
with orchestral harmony.

Then a sudden rain,
like the force of a pebble,
strikes my wide hat.

You laugh,
pushing up the limp brim.
Kiss me.

Don't

Don't write a love poem, I say.
The kind that makes some readers wince,
but you fill me with something I can't quite comprehend.
I'm speaking phrases
So heavy they're almost foreign:
The day you left, the sun vanished.
Trite maybe, but true.

Don't write of things others can't picture.
That's what I say, too,
yet you were so handsome outside the embassy.
You offered the elbow of your blue uniform
as we stepped into the ballroom.

Not that I need anything to remind me of you,
not even your cassettes, your guitar,
knowing you're far in the distance.

And for God's sake, don't speculate,
Not with tired metaphors.
How can I not say that day was scripted,
listening to 'Broken Wings' –
it's tragic love.
Our young voices still vibrate,
learning to fly on the wind.

Don't say any more.
Just don't.
I put down the pen.

Poems have words, but some say nothing.
I thought you might not speak,
but you did.

Terminal

'Ping!'

I'm there again
every time I step through an airport.

Twenty-two, naïve,
stopped at Hong Kong security.
Thinking only
of Hong Kong dollars
and tacky souvenirs.

I am taken to a room.
I say something,
but my voice comes from a place
I don't recognise.
His eyes hold mine,
questions I can't understand.
Something about diamonds.
I have visions
of wasting my life in a squalid prison
for something I know nothing about.

These things happen, you know.
They do.

After two hours of sweats and questions,
shaken heads and accusations,
he lets loose a sarcastic smirk,
opens his office door.
I am free to leave.

Despite all the years that have passed,
I still see him, hear that voice,
authoritative, stern,
'Where's the diamond?'

Dancing Scorpions

We are riding camels eastwards,
the sun is high, settled
like a fierce creature on our faces
The sand seems to hum
with the drumming of the wind.

Under the Argan tree, a smiling man
whose face is wet with sweat,
crushes seeds to extract their oil,
until suddenly his rough hands
tugs on my bright red shawl
to use it to frame my head and face
just like a Berber.

From his pocket he takes
three brown scorpions,
dancing circles in a bottle.
He drops them onto my hand,
and I pray that they won't bite.
Through my arm, a flood of shivers
but then a kind of calm, as if
these scurrying things were my own children.

He has taught me, this man,
who has no camels to impress generous tourists.
He has taught me to be free –
of what I have yet to understand.

Aging Mist

From fragments of corals and shells,
I picked up a round, grey pebble
wishing to dab my feet in another ocean.

My memories
were transoceanic,
swelling like musical peaks.

And all the years,
I've walked by the sea,
you painted on every pebble.

Restless brown eyes,
silvered hair grown wild,
white seaweed-ragged beard fluttering,
cruising the Andaman,
your cracked fingers like spiders
on the saxophone,
every note, pure.
Your playing is warm,
spinning
our favourite song –

Memories are mist,
even on a clear day.

Whores! You Shame Our Country

Fresh falafel beneath Tunisian sky.

Chests disrobed for revolt.
This collective voice
grasps history and straddles continents,
court tragedies and triumphs.

Slogans speak on painted chests:
'Breasts feed revolution,'
Can you hear their potent language?
'Free Amina!'

Storm-faced policemen push
through the crowd,
ferret eyes darting.

Confident, pretty, full-breasted,
controversy sparks,
the media glares.

Yet, everyone wants
to stare.

Soon their names, too,
will be carved
in the prison book.

France 24 June 12 2013: Tunisia sentences Femen topless activists to prison.

Separation Wall

for Ahed Tamimi, teenage freedom fighter

A keffiyeh scarf around her neck,
she is a symbol,
with a voice.

'I protest now and forever,' she says.
Words repeated whenever anyone
looks on the huge mural of her face
that crosses the divide,
between Palestine and Israel.
One land ailing,
the other fattening.

Despite the machine guns and air strikes
that plunder the schools and homes around her,
there is little bitterness
in a voice that has known
eight months of imprisonment for slapping a soldier,
who shot her cousin in the face,
'I want to see peace without borders,
without occupation.'

Others have said
the ultimate evil
is knowing wrong,
and looking away.
These are words
without a face,

words that somehow drift in our minds,
that seemed always to exist,
ancient as cave paintings,
greed or hate.

'I ask you now –
what
are
you
going
to do?'

Her face questions those who pass it,
those who view it on a distant screen.

**Ahed's imprisonment sparked international condemnation
shone a spotlight on children prisoners in Israeli jails.*

We Want Another Life

I remember the day, dazed
by a wall of dark cloud,
mother digging through piles
of rubble with bare hands
to save the man she loved.

Here darkening German fields
    lit by blue cornflowers,
a long way
from the constant smell
of burnt flesh.

On the fresh-scented earth,
I lie down – picture
the jasmine in our garden,
it's white stars, the sun
sprinkling turmeric in the sky.

Prisoner 46664, Robben Island

for Mandela

I had a chance to return
to where I had spent
eighteen years in captivity,
a 7 x 9 foot room.
I could walk the length of my cell in three paces.

Where I had missed
births and funerals,
weddings and anniversaries –
I wanted to reach those I love,
but many had gone.

Voices overlapped,
but thoughts
ran like a clear stream
over rough sediment,

and I asked myself,
What more can you do?
But pray and hope,
pray and hope.

Here, I recalled a warden's first words:
'This is where you will die.'

In the Room of Marie Fogarty

from 'An Apology for Roses'

The moon,
cuts a silhouette of him,
bent,
as he removes
the stiff white collar,
to place a handkerchief,
over the Blessed Virgin
in the young girl's room.

In the empty house,
while her parents are at mass,
she has pursued him,
till all his resistance, weakening.

The muted sounds of bedsprings,
are beasts howling in the dark,

their contrasting worlds,
brushed against each other,
just as her body brushed,
many times, against new visitors.

His spirit is worn,
like a grotto in the rain.

Closure

Vincent Harney's voice
comes over the airwaves –
his 44 years as Postmaster will cease,
a family's 60 years at Cornafulla Post Office
tapering like a country lane
succumbing to grass.

When I see him,
I tell him,
I am the daughter of a postmaster.

We talk of pre-digital days,
him a young telegram boy
delivering 'rush' messages
of joy, success or sorrow.
Dreading the task
of conveying bad news.

I can't quite let go of faces I meet here,
to collect money, stamp our envelopes –
I can't imagine where we'll meet again.

A new chapter will begin for Vincent,
farming land, working bog
and the urge to travel.

Vincent stands in the doorway.
'Well', he sighs,
'It's all settled.'

A Mini Forest of Hazel Triskele

for Deirdre Hannon

Here at Lough Ree –
The spring breeze whistles off the lake
tossing the hawthorn's shiny green leaves.
Swans arch their wings,
windsurfing across the water,
the air purrs with butterflies and bees,
and the *king of the forest,*
a huge handsome oak
shades the Triskele.

She kneels on the grass,
hears the sound of the earth keening.
She offers a prayer
and spreads tobacco on the ground.

She travels to every county,
creating a mini forest
of the same triple-spiralled template,
urging it to grow.
Meanwhile she walks her meditations around it,
thirty-three hazels for peace,
a single birch for new beginnings,
bluebells and anemones,
ringed with stones rescued from the sea.

Remedies

Here in the country
roaring verdant wild nettles,
hymn the air, an invitation to harvest.

My neighbour, Mary explains,
'Nettles are the best treatment for arthritis.
Grasp the plant in a gloved hand,
swat them on stiff joints.
This practice, called urtication
dates back two thousand years.'

Papa told me of many remedies –

cinnamon in boiled water,
to relieve aching muscles,
betel leaf to stop nosebleeds,
ginger for a healthy heart,
turmeric paste spread on the face,
to calm unruly skin.

In my suburban kitchen,
in a large wok filled with boiled rice,
sliced okra and crushed garlic,
fuse with an unfussed hush.
It simmers to a dance
of translucent onions.
My daughters will taste fried rice,
tinged with chatters

of ginger and scallions,
I'll scoop steamed nettles onto their plates,
imagine them filter
through their growing bodies.

Poet-Gardener

Grousing under his breath
beneath burnt sienna leaves,
an intimate battle,
a day searching
for sunlight
through burgeoning clouds.

The muse
is present,
with flawless skin, perfumed,
bending
lacy skirted before his hand,
which offers seeds to eager birds,
while his foot shoos rabbits away.

When the sun strays
through the gap of haughty conifers,
it drags with it
a pair of lines
that reek of a scent
he's worn before,

a brand of perfection,
moulded in the moment.

He raises the brim of his fedora,
runs his hands through his platinum beard.
The soil-brown tips of his fingers

will shift about the shaft of a pen,
nimble as a spider
wrapping its prey.

With a Capital C

Her nose wrinkles,
as if she senses
a putrid smell,
from this new thing
squatting inside her.

'I'm not going to give it a name,' she says,
suspended
somewhere between
refusal
and denial.

She lies on a couch,
curled up like an embryo,
and repeats the letters,
'C! C! C!'
or perhaps she means 'See! See! See!'
a sonata of strangeness
stretching into the afternoon.

At the bathroom mirror,
she wipes her eyes,
pats on a cream
to conceal dark circles
like bruised aubergines.

She reaches into her bra,
filling the empty half
with a cold, oval foam.

Seeing Rain

for my brother; a chef, a painter and singer

Days before,
on a Skype call
patchy as a Spanish field,

he told me he'd chosen
to die before
death could choose him first.

'Do you remember
the song I played?' he asked
through talk of our teenage years.

His face had become our father's face.
and three days later his throat too
carried no air.

I am left
his recipes, his art, his Levi's,
his borrowed songs,

I take now for myself, mumbling:
'Have you ever
seen the rain?'

She of the Two Faces

I watch my husband
draw the blinds with one hand,
hold a cigarette with the other.
He smiles,
Mesmerised.
His gaze wandering across the garden.

Often he stands at the glass door,
checks the time on his wristwatch.

When night arrives,
I close the blinds,
but he reopens, to catch a new glimpse
before retiring,
wondering if she's lost a second,
like a needle dropping a stitch.

In the cold hours,
I ask myself should I feel insecure?

But somehow, I don't mind sharing him
with the double-face hanging
on the stone well in our garden.
The stylish Miss Paddington
adds personality to our exterior.

After all,
it is I he turns to at night.

Care Guide for Pablo

I

Therefore,
bowls must be full to last through the day till evening,
dry food mainly; Whiskas tuna tasty filled pockets.
Feed him only when he comes inside
after playing with Ginger.
Wet food should be given occasionally.
The water bowl must always be full,
and be sure to allow for evaporation.

II

The litter box:
Poo should be scooped into a pink plastic bag.
If it smells bad, sprinkle a layer of fresh litter in the box.
If very stinky, fill the box with the fresh litter.
And don't forget to bin the bag.

III

At all times, keep the utility door open.
Close the windows.
And if he happens to wander outside,
just wait for him to return.
After an hour has elapsed,
call out his name in a pleasant tone.

(Imagine you're happily married to him).
He is sure to expect cuddles, and throwing treats
around the room, is always a nice touch.

IV

When you can't find Pablo, don't panic.
Check:
(a) behind couch in the conservatory.
(b) in your bathroom.
(c) on Yasmine's bed or Natasya's bed, under the covers.
(d) on dining room chairs or the cupboard by the stairs.
(e) or trapped in a closet with the door closed.

After your day's work, remember to greet him by his name,
in a voice that's warm, with a rounded feel, cosy
like a blanket wrapped around him, one that touches his heart.

Music Flows on the Marble Island

Pablo, my tuxedo cat,
listens to Neruda's
Clenched Soul, on YouTube.
Then he prances about
to *Lady Hear Me Tonight*.

I am curled on a couch
with pomegranate juice,
and chocolate-dipped strawberries,
contemplating another poem –

A handsome Malayan tiger,
eyes amber, irises black as burnt clay.
He roars like a high-speed train
on the marble island.

But I am a culchie on a sunset prowl,
insatiable as hot Mary,
I flirt with tigers.
Turn the pages of my notes,
and write hormone-fuelled dreams.

Showtime

Of social indiscretion and unfortunate times,
Annie talks,
sitting, with legs crossed high
at the dressing table.
Her braceleted arm dangles
over a high-back chair,
a thick cigar between her fingers.
She breaks into a laugh as we chat.
Her voice husky, as if weighed down
with summer heat.

Soft straight hair,
a precisely wielded eyebrow pencil,
another brush of mascara,
chilli-red lipstick,
gold-painted nails,
24- inch waist,
in slinky, scarlet cheongsam,
these pert breasts,
belong in this body,
whose skin is the colour of honey.

A pretty boy, they call her on the street,
refusing to accept her.

A head in the door says, 'You're going on, Miss.'
She stands,
assuredly 'she'.

Convent Girl

'Simple in virtue, Steadfast in duty'
— *School motto*

I entered primary school at the Convent,
named after Father Barre, a prolific writer
and inspiring teacher to the Sisters.
Our progress tightly monitored
by the no-nonsense nuns.

Pupils of different religions and cultural backgrounds
were placed in the same classroom.
Christian teachers and pupils said their prayers
at morning assemblies, Muslim pupils
attended separate religious classes.

Straight-trunk rubber trees surrounded the school,
dispersed pale brown seeds became
figurines of ants, caterpillars,
their see-through dried leaves
became dragonfly wings.

Sports day, the chance to ditch our feminine manners,
we turned cartwheels and somersaults,
competed in high jumps, long jumps.
We ran in gunny sacks,
and tip-toed on hairy coconut shells.

There was a thistle of noise from the all-boys school:
  'Convent girls are very cheap,
    five cents for a kiss, ten for a sleep ...'

And now ... 'Convent girls are very cheap,
    Five cents for a kiss, ten for a sleep.'
    Not a hope! We are Convent girls.'

At Father Barre Convent

'Heel and toe, heel and toe,
slide, slide, slide ...'
Her long skirt billowing,
her veil flapping about her shoulders.
Sister George, a young Irish nun
shone when she spoke,
naming all the folk dance moves.
The taller girl took the role of the 'gentleman'.

One very hot day, my nose bled.
Sister George squeezed a betel leaf
to my nose.
At her quarters, thrilled at the treats
she gave me,
feigned being ill yet again.

Sister Agnes with her clipped
English accent,
taught us to pronounce the words,
'Mother ... Father ...' –
the tip of her tongue lifted
to a fogged-up mirror,
to show the difference,
she would say, 'Not Maader or Faader.'

I had the same partner till second class.
We were taught
to help each other in our studies.

If one forgot her times tables or homework,
her partner would be punished.
I felt the painful lash of Sister Agnes's ruler,
many times more
than my partner.

The Curse of Guilt

For years, I suppressed the thought:
was it I, somehow, who was responsible?
I still remember my curse,
the fusillade of questions.
Why did he have to take my car
instead of leaving on his motorbike?

He said he was going to a café,
but he was bent on partying with friends.
Lately, I found him sleeping at the site.
Not exactly a model employee.
'You go to hell … You …
Go and die!'

Next day, I heard the news.
I sat down to stop myself from trembling,
couldn't undo the images
twisting in my mind.
Maybe that curve in the road …
he just didn't see it coming.

I couldn't sleep for months,
kept seeing him there,
slumped over the cracked steering wheel,
the horn blaring, one arm
out the window, just the way he drove.

Tower Site Inspection at Esso Refinery

My hands are pure white,
perspiration falls from my helmet.
The steel ladder stretches below,
a hundred feet.
A glance down, and it becomes meandering ropes.

The instrument engineer touches my hand,
'Boss, don't look down.
Concentrate on the steps.'
We descend,
some men have failed,
hours marooned at the top
until another, more assured,
escorted them to the ground.
Though slow,
I am determined.

My gaze is fixed on the distant sea.
The Strait of Malacca glows, sunset
like a flame of the forest
blooming outside my window.

My head spins,
my boots suddenly heavier,
both hands firm on the ladder.
I measure out slow, controlled steps.

On the ground,
I slide the sweat-filled gloves from my fingers,
grasp the hot red earth.
Their eyes tell me a woman
needs time to recover,

but I dust off my hands
and tell my engineers to get their hands dirty
I pull out a pen
and complete the report.